'Wellbeing is realised by small steps, but is truly no small thing.'

– Zeno of Citium

Unlocking my Greatest Self

For the many challenges and people
(you know who you are) that have given me
strength and invaluable learnings.

David Osborn-Cook

www.DOCwellness.co.uk

Copyright © 2024 by David P Osborn-Cook. All rights reserved.

No portion of this book may be reproduced, stored or transmitted in any form or by any means, electronic, mechanical, photocopying, recording or scanning, or otherwise without written permission from the publisher or author. It is illegal to copy this book, post it to a website, or distribute it by any other means without permission.

This publication is designed to provide accurate and authoritative information in regard to the subject matter covered. While the publisher and author have used their best efforts in preparing this book, they make no representations or warranties with respect to the accuracy or completeness of the contents of this book and specifically disclaim any implied warranties of merchantability or fitness for a particular purpose. No warranty may be created or extended by sales representatives or written sales materials. The advice and strategies contained herein may not be suitable for your situation. You should consult with a professional when appropriate. Neither the publisher nor the author shall be liable for any loss of profit or any other commercial damages, including but not limited to special, incidental, consequential, personal, or other damages.

2nd Edition 2024. Typography and Design by Mick Tonello. www.micktonello.com

ISBN 978-1-8365-4241-4

Published by **Streaming Leaves Books**

Contents

Introduction from me, David

Chapter One: Out of Anxiety and Stress

- No. 1:   Is that Thought True? Really?
- No. 2:   Be NOWhere Right Now
- No. 3:   The Never Make Things Worse Rule
- No. 4:   Hey You! Snap Out of Yourself
- No. 5:   Nothing Lasts. Even Bad Feelings
- No. 6:   Newsflash! Watch Less News
- No. 7:   Are You Constantly Must-urbating?
- No. 8:   Thoughts Floating Downstream
- No. 9:   Accept Anxiety and Become Awareness
- No. 10: Never Fear Fear, Just do It
- No. 11: Are You Negatively Self-Hypnotising?
- No. 12: Build Resilience. Inoculate Yourself

Chapter Two: Towards Confidence and Assertiveness

- No. 13: Stop Ruminating, Start Living
- No. 14: Nothing Compares to You. So Don't
- No. 15: Reframe to a Positive Mindset

No. 16: Calm. Sweet Effortless Calm
No. 17: From Self-Conscious to Powerful
No. 18: Reboot Yourself Now
No. 19: Be Bold, be Assertive, be You
No. 20　Ha Ha Ha Laugh at Yourself
No. 21: How to Take Criticism
No. 22: Slowww Down. Pull People in

Chapter Three: Becoming Superhuman
No. 23: What's Your Story? Let's Start a New Chapter
No. 24: Are You Living Your Values?
No. 25: Neuroplasticity and Rewiring Your Life
No. 26: Get Good at Something. Get Brilliant
No. 27: Feel the Music, Feel Alive
No. 28: Treat Every Person as a VIP
No. 29: Choose Your Experience
No. 30: Six Habits for Success
No. 31: Everything has a Cost / Benefit
No. 32: Stop Trying to Sleep and Sleep

Chapter Four: Living in Wisdom
No. 33: Anger Kills You, Not Them
No. 34: The Inestimable Power of Gratitude

No. 35: Change Yourself First. Then the World
No. 36: Accept What You Cannot Change
No. 37: Practise Loving Yourself and Beyond
No. 38: Treat Failure as Feedback
No. 39: Forgive and Suffer No More
No. 40: What Are You Ignoring?
No. 41: Spread a Kindness Epidemic
No. 42: Stop the Incessant Judgment

Chapter Five: Spirituality and a Little Magic

No. 43: Ego or Infinite Consciousness?
No. 44: How to Be Constantly Happy
No. 45: Becoming Nature Again
No. 46: Synchronicity and the OMG Factor
No. 47: Your Imagination is King. Be Careful!
No. 48: Co-create Using the Quantum Field
No. 49: Mad, Unwavering Faith
No. 50: The Power of I Am

Index

About me, the Author

An introduction from me, *David*.

About you

My guess is you picked up this book because you're smart, inquisitive, ambitious ... and anxious to know how to survive and thrive on this beautiful, uncertain planet.

Maybe you're even **actually** anxious. (And God knows there's enough to be anxious about.)

Maybe you want to learn how to cope better, grow – but don't have time to wade through lots of esoteric books.

Maybe you want some deep, but simply-put solutions that work.

Nuggets, practical exercises and beyond

With that in mind, I've compiled these 50 short wisdom and therapeutic 'nuggets' – with practical exercises. A playbook for life, if you like.

They've been inspired directly by my work as a professional Hypno-CBT therapist, life coach and my spiritual and philosophical readings. Also by my own struggles and challenges.

For me, therapy alone isn't enough. So, yes there are solid, science-based therapeutic ideas and practices here, but there are also some further insights that wander into other disciplines.

Because when you start looking deeper, things open up and you start seeing connections – between all kinds of things.

Go as far as you want

Look into these nuggets and look further.

You can go from anxiety … and build yourself up towards some kind of resilience, confidence, peace, happiness – and even sneak a glimpse of enlightenment.

You can cross-refer using the index at the back. So you can take a journey. But you don't have to. You can dip in, dip out at will. You'll still learn something and experience a shift.

Keep exploring, keep practising, practising, practising

Of course, these nuggets are a taster. They are distilled, crunched down. So please explore them elsewhere in more detail.

There are familiar ideas, 'secret' ideas (depending on what you've read) and 'out there' ideas (depending on your viewpoint). And you'll discover similarities and repetition as you go (connections again).

I'd like to think there's some real gold here.

If you do spend time learning and practising the processes, you might just find yourself growing into that amazing person everyone wants to spend time with and love ... including you.

Keep it up – and keep going. Make it a habit. And slowly (and gently) you may even contribute to changing this planet we share.

Enjoy.

This book is deliberately aesthetically pleasing – to bring the words and ideas to life and help the concepts stick deep. For that I am hugely indebted to the magnificent Mick Tonello, who has patience and talent in abundance. Many thanks to Mick in Sydney, Australia.   www.micktonello.com

Out of
Anx
and

Chapter No. 1.

iety
Stress

Is that Thought True? Really?

№ 1.

Let's start with the cruel lies we often tell ourselves. 'I'm hopeless', 'I'll never be any good'. But these thoughts are distortions and projections, not facts. We catastrophise and generalise – leading to anxiety, depression. Stop this now.

DO THIS

1. Start to write down your negative thoughts. Maybe keep a journal.
2. Is that true? Give each thought a rating out of 100% for how much you **really** believe it.
3. Write next to that thought which emotion it causes and the intensity out of 100%.
4. Then write a better, more practical thought instead and re-rate your belief in the original one – and how much your emotion has changed.

No. 2.

Nothing exists but the Now. Yet some things are hard to shake off – past musings, the future and its 'what ifs'. In learning to be more present, anxieties drop and we can become calmer, re-centred and enjoy the beauty of the divine moment.

DO THIS

The 4-3-2-1 method for recentring.

1. Close your eyes and open them. **Look** at 4 different things very closely for 30 seconds each.
2. Close your eyes and **listen** for 4 things similarly.
3. **Feel** 4 things on your skin, like your shirt collar.
4. Begin again doing 3 for each sense, then 2 each, then one.
5. Treat your day more like this.

BE NOWhere RIGHT Now

THE Never make things worse RULE

No. 3.

People say, 'it is what it is', right? And it actually is. Until WE decide to make something of it, put a meaning on it, a thought. We can turn a straightforward situation into a problem, a discussion into an argument. Everything can snowball.

DO THIS

1. Stop yourself! In these moments, take that life-saving breath and step back. Be AWARENESS. (See No. 9).
2. Are you making more of this than you need? Think about it. How bad is this event, this issue, really? Ask yourself, 'what's the worst that could happen?'
3. Let the air out, keep the issue to the size of a golf ball, don't inflate it to a football by adding more emotions to it.

No. 4.

We spend 95% of our precious day on autopilot, in sub-conscious habits, our own semi-hypnotic state. And 60% of our thinking is apparently negative or self-sabotaging. Time to WAKE UP, don't you think, and turn things around?

DO THIS

1. Get a bright, cool elastic band and put it on your wrist.
2. Every time you notice an intrusive negative thought creep in, ping it.
3. Feel the pain! And change that thought or action around to a positive.
4. What else could you be thinking? Think!

Hey You! Snap out of yourself

Nothing lasts. Even bad feelings

No. 5.

There are certain moments we want to last forever. But nothing does – and that has a positive side, because when you feel down, that goes too. Remember, you are NOT your feelings or thoughts – they are transient, like passing clouds.

DO THIS

1. Find a quiet place. Close your eyes and remember a time and place when you felt calm, happy, confident.
2. Really look around, at the colours and shapes, listen to the sounds, feel the temperature. Get deeper into the feelings.
3. Pinch your *left thumb* and *first two fingers* together. This is your anchoring. Breathe in, hold for 5, breathe out slowly, go deeper ...
4. Repeat and embed the above. You can bring these feelings back any time with this anchoring action.

No. 6.

From a mental health perspective the news is an unnecessary agent of anxiety. Yes it's good to be informed, but information is only useful if you can act on it – and often we can't. Know this, let any guilt go and be free.

DO THIS

1. If you're drawn to certain news stories and are worrying about what has happened, or might happen, stop.
2. Check to see if you can do anything to change or improve the events.
3. Maybe you can join a political party, go on a march or campaign for your cause.
4. If you can't act, and you're highly anxious, it's best to work on weaning yourself off the news entirely. Turn off or turn over.

Newsflash! Watch LESS News

Are YOU constantly must-urbating?

No. 7.

Albert Ellis, co-founder of CBT, came up with the phrase, Must-urbating. Whenever you think sentences beginning with the words, 'I must ...', or 'I should ...' or 'I need ...' beware! You're putting unnecessary pressure on yourself.

DO THIS

1. Watch yourself closely for I need/should/must thoughts and distance yourself from them.
2. Remember, these kind of thoughts have likely come from peers, work, social media, past parental pressure, schooling ... but mainly ourselves for allowing them into our unconscious.
3. Let go. Practise mindfulness and look to No. 8 overleaf.

No. 8.

Our thoughts can literally be the death of us. As we've seen in No. 1, our stories and hypotheses are often untrue. Recognise the negativity. You can question those thoughts or you can also let them pass by with a gentle relaxing meditation.

DO THIS

1. Close your eyes and imagine you are walking in the countryside, alone. It's a nice bright autumn day and you see ahead of you a river.

2. Watch as leaves fall from a tree on the bank opposite and settle on the surface of the river. Watch these leaves pass downstream.

3. When a random thought pops up ... put it on the leaf (imagine it written on a piece of paper) and LET IT GO. Repeat for 10 minutes with any thought that emerges. Use this idea with negative thoughts in the day.

thoughts *floating* Down stream

Accept Anxiety and become Awareness

No. 9.

Anxiety seems to lurk behind every corner we turn. We worry about our identity, the environment, economic uncertainty, conflict, our own expectations. But the secret is – don't fight anything. Accept and allow ... and, incredibly, things change.

DO THIS

1. Take a moment. Say 'hello' to your negative feelings, open your arms and accept them in – as normal, harmless and transient.
2. Then step back, watch things from a distance as The Observer. Rehearse yourself being in control as if you've achieved calmness.
3. Repeat the above as a habit.
4. It helps to ask, 'Am I that feeling, or am I the one who is aware of it?'

No. 10.

Fear can keep us safe – but it can stop us living a full, expanded life. It's often the result of one bad experience generalised –or an overactive imagination. Step forward and be bold. There's a reason Nike used the slogan, 'Just do it'.

DO THIS

1. Avoidance is a bad tactic. Face your fear. Look it in the eye, be endlessly curious.
2. If it's a snake, look at the wonderful shape and colours.
3. If it's a speech, sit with the anxiety for a moment ... then rehearse it going well in your mind.
4. Take some slow gentle deep breaths, get yourself into relaxation and really imagine it going well. Keep going.

Never fear Fear, Just do it

Are you *negatively* SELF-hypnotising?

No. 11.

Hypnosis is simply a state of focusing on something and ignoring everything else. A fixation. We do it watching TV, in groups, in politics, sport, anything. Do it with our own negative thoughts and we can become down or anxious.

DO THIS

1. Try to gain perspective. Remain open and Aware.
2. Ask this, 'What am I ignoring or forgetting?'
3. Consider other angles, whether you're caught in your own negative self-hypnosis (bad and unfounded thoughts about yourself), an argument or ideology.
4. Open up to the positive, consider gratitude (No. 34).

No. 12.

In western society we find ourselves constantly in competition, with high expectations – win, lose, win etc. It's not a natural habitat for calmness and co-operation. If we're to survive, let alone thrive, we need to learn how to cope with the game.

DO THIS

1. NEVER avoid pressure. Resilience is built by facing up to it in stages – like building a muscle.
2. Think of it like inoculating yourself ... taking a little bit on increases your immunity.
3. So drop your fears, act like it's all normal, accept the feelings and welcome them in.

Build resilience. Inoculate yourself

Towards
Confi
and Asse

Chapter No. 2.

dence
rtiveness

STOP
ruminating,
START
living

No. 13.

Rumination is living in the past – and can lead to depression. Pondering setbacks, grievances and regrets can seriously damage your mood, polluting your experience of what could be a glorious present moment – and future.

DO THIS

1. It sounds obvious, but the past is over. Recognise it's an illusion, a story you're throwing meaning onto.
2. If you can do something, do it. Act. If it's a person troubling you, reach out or unfollow them, perhaps. Try a new action.
3. If it's something you can't do, distract yourself. Identify what triggers you, write it down. And be mindful.

No. 14.

Looks, wealth, career, relationships, health. There's always someone better or better off than you in every corner of life. Why compare? Why set yourself up for disappointment and unhappiness when there's another way?

DO THIS

1. If you're feeling down, instead of looking at others, look at yourself and only yourself.
2. Compare yourself with how **you** were **yesterday**. Are you happier? Have you made a step in the right direction?
3. Make sure your today is better than it was yesterday by doing something you didn't do yesterday. Repeat that idea tomorrow. That way, you're always headed north!

Nothing compares TO YOU. So don't

Reframe to a Positive mindset

No. 15.

We can easily get stuck in a specific mode of thinking.
But it's often simply an angle of perception,
a viewpoint developed from past experiences.
We end up projecting our own beliefs onto situations.
It might be useful to reframe things.

DO THIS

1. Expand your Awareness. Everything can be viewed another way if we step beyond ourselves.

2. Consider this: you're driving and the car in front is going too slow for your comfort. Recognise your feelings – think wider.

3. Maybe the person is old, or recovering from an accident. Maybe it's time you learned to slow down too – for everyone's sake!

4. Always ask yourself, is there **a more useful** way of looking at this?

No. 16.

Watch any elite sportsperson, musician or actor.
They have one thing in common; they're totally relaxed.
Effortless. Flowing. Getting out of their own way.
This is the sweet spot where good health and
everything amazing happens.

DO THIS

1. Take a break every two hours. Close your eyes, breathe in deeply and sharply through the nose, filling your lungs.
2. Hold for 10 secs. Let the air out slowly through pursed lips for 12 seconds. And say to yourself on the outbreath, 'I am becoming calm, relaxed and confident' ... and think of a quiet, calm place.
3. Repeat for 2 minutes.
4. Do this regularly and see your health and general performance pick up.

Calm.
Sweet effortless
Calm

from **self-conscious to Powerful**

No. 17.

We can all feel awkward and self-conscious at times. But it's possible to move beyond ourselves and our inhibitions towards that special **flow** state. Especially when talking in groups or in public – towards expression, confidence and power.

DO THIS

1. Always look outward! When in a social group or public speaking, focus OUT not in.
2. Look at items on people's clothes in detail, their features whilst talking or listening. The shapes and colours of things around.
3. Widen your peripheral vision occasionally. Take yourself out of yourself, get flowing and be involved. Rehearse, rehearse, rehearse in your mind – this is working from 'in vitro' (testing) to 'in vivo' (life).

No. 18.

Feeing bored, unenthusiastic, low or listless? Learn something new. It will kick-start you and reactivate your motivation. Give yourself up to it entirely. Day after day. Bit by bit. Until you master it ... and yourself.

DO THIS

1. Choose something you like the sound of, the feel of, the look of, the taste of; what you can get passionate about.
2. Maybe it's a particular musical instrument, or a new language, a sport, a dance, mountaineering.
3. Devote yourself to it. And get really good at it.
4. Alternatively, if you're learning something smaller, like baking or cooking, pick something different every week.

Reboot yourself NOW

be **Bold,** be assertive, be **You**

No. 19.

You were born to be you. As the famous 1927 poem, 'Desiderata' says, 'You are a child of the Universe ... you have a right to be here' (Max Ehrmann). So shrink from nothing, fear nothing and unleash your creativity – to manifest your higher self.

DO THIS

1. Come out with what you think and feel. Take a risk.
2. Be Aware of course, of the situation. Make an assessment. But don't hold back.
3. If you're normally self-conscious, practise being more spontaneous and expressive – in your face and with your hands.
4. Observe others' behaviours throughout the day.
5. Do something unusual each week: wear a loud hat on the train ... or sing aloud! ;–)

No. 20.

Laughter is an intoxicating medicine. It lightens, lifts and reframes otherwise heavy situations. And if you can laugh at yourself, it's disarming, signals humility and confidence ... and can draw people to you. Welcome to the charisma factor.

DO THIS

1. Watch interviews with celebrities like Ryan Reynolds and Jennifer Lawrence. There are loads more.
2. Notice how being self-deprecating can be strangely charismatic and get people onside and laughing too.
3. The moment you find yourself shamed by something, or saying something silly, pull yourself up. And laugh openly.

Ha Ha Ha
Laugh
AT
yourself

HOW to take Criticism

No. 21.

Reacting badly to criticism by defending yourself in an unholy manner actually diminishes you in others' eyes and loses you the very thing you wanted – respect. It shows immaturity and lack of self-worth. Mind those emotions.

DO THIS

1. Notice that (often familiar) feeling within you rising when you're about to react to something someone says or does.
2. Shrug off that 'getting defensive-ness'. Know that there may be some merit in a criticism and take it on board.
3. Behave lightly, calmly and gracefully because your self-esteem is strong.
4. Truly confident people know that there's nothing they can possibly lose at a psychological level.

No. 22.

Have you noticed, time seems to move slower for certain people? Their won't-be-hurried demeanour sends a powerful signal to others of their confidence and standing. This relaxed aura magnetically and magically pulls people to them.

DO THIS

1. So, yes, consciously slow down. Take your time. Be reeeaally calm.
2. If you think this is easy, try it. You'll find your mind will be rushing around wanting to appease or impart something.
3. Practise leaving gaps in your sentences, some air, slow your words and ... be quieter.
4. Watch people lean in to you to listen to your words.
5. Don't rush food ... or anything else either!

Slowww down. pull PEOPLE in

Becoming Sup

Chapter No. 3.

er
human

What's your story? Let's start a new Chapter

No. 23.

Everything is story. What's happened to us, what we tell ourselves – about our past, our achievements and so called 'failings'. It's all about how we interpret these events, how we often fictionalise them. Time for a plot twist.

DO THIS

1. Don't let the past pattern your present and your future. The past is only to learn from, it doesn't have to control you.

2. So be AWARE. Recognise the events and feelings unfolding. Write them down. Draw a line under them all.

3. Write 'Chapter NOW.' And start drafting some new goals and imagine them happening – in depth. Play around with this idea and revisit daily.

No. 24.

Do you feel lethargic or unfulfilled? Maybe you're spending your time doing things you feel you 'have to', rather than things you love. That's drudgery and a signal that you need to reappraise your life and reapportion your time better.

DO THIS

1. Write out 8 value areas as follows: Friends & Family, Marriage/Partners, Money, Career, Personal Growth, Fun & Leisure, Community, Health/Wellbeing.
2. Rate each on how important they are to you out of 20.
3. Rate how successfully you've lived this value in the last month (out of 20).
4. Rank them in order of how important it is to work on that one right now (1 to 8). Assess.
5. For more on values, search 'Wheel of Life.'

Are you *Living* your *Values?*

Neuroplasticity and rewiring your Life

No. 25.

'Neurons that fire together, wire together' (Donald O. Hebb, 1949). So, keep repeating a thought, emotion or action, and your brain's pathways get hardwired. It's why we fall into the same moods or anxieties. Welcome to Neuroplasticity.

DO THIS

1. Neuroscience tells us that if we practise positive thinking or behaviours enough times, we can write over the negative neural pathways we've created before.

2. If you're experiencing anxiety, for instance, practise gratitude or positive thought repetition and you can start to change your mood and outlook.

3. Do positive activities more often, research this idea and get into more useful habits.

No. 26.

Being average is ... a bit average, let's face it. Nothing wrong with that. But wouldn't it be nice to be really good at something? The guitar, shearing sheep, gurning or even listening ... yes listening!
Commit yourself to something. Anything.

DO THIS

1. What do you like doing? Have a think.
2. Whatever it is, just stick to it every day and practise it.
3. Throw yourself into it heart and soul. You'll master that thing ... and lose yourself.
4. You'll then know HOW to be good at something ... and you can do that with something else ... and something else.

get **Good** at something. Get *brilliant*

Feel *the* Music, *feel* Alive

No. 27.

If music be the food of love, play on! (Shakespeare, of course). Music is a tangible force that has the power to enhance and transform emotions. Go to any gig and just feel the vibe and energy. It heals, connects and uplifts like nothing else.

DO THIS

1. If you're listless, low or feeling disconnected, become aware of that feeling.
2. Think of your favourite artists, singers, bands that connect you to some of your best times.
3. Search, press play. Feel it, sing it, dance it!
4. Compile the 'Tracks of Your Life' – ones that trigger some lovely moments.
5. Or experiment with something unknown – e.g. Mozart, Gregorian chant or rap. Vary it up.

No. 28.

You'd like to be popular. You want to be liked, understood and appreciated. Of course you do. But life is reciprocal. Be interested in yourself first, and improving yourself. And be interested in everyone you meet. Every single one.

DO THIS

1. Every time you meet someone, treat that person like they're the only person in the room.
2. Look them in the eye, listen to their every word and really engage with them.
3. Subtly mirror their language and their gestures ... you might find yourself doing that anyhow. It's rapport. But be mindful you're not mimicking them!

Treat Every person as a VIP

Choose your Experience

No. 29.

In adversity you always have a choice. Give in to negativity – and make things worse. Or you can choose to experience that situation differently. With positivity and gusto perhaps. That way lies heroism ... and a possible miracle!

DO THIS

1. If something happens in your life – an accident, an illness, a failed exam or relationship – first **accept** what you can't change.

2. Be willing to change your **experience** of it. Allow yourself 5 minutes of negativity.

3. Then strive to be perhaps the **happiest, most positive** person who has experienced that event.

4. See what changes that sparks in your life.

No. 30.

According to research, there are six habitual activities that the most successful, contented people do. Many start these but give up early, seeking the new trendy quick fix. But stick to those below and your life will change. Guaranteed.

DO THIS

1. Meditation. See No. 8, for instance, and take 5–15 mins out.
2. Affirmations. See various nuggets in this book.
3. Visualisation. Many are in this book – really focus and feel.
4. Exercise. The obvious. Do 30 mins a day.
5. Reading. Set aside an hour or more a day. Educate yourself and get that imagination going.
6. Journalling. Write down your negative thoughts, ideas and things you can improve on. See the various journaling in this book.

Six habits FOR Success

Everything has a Cost/benefit

No. 31.

Every action or decision has some kind of cost and a benefit to consider. Everything we do. Everything that happens. An awkward chat with the boss. Rain. Social media – politicians, surgeons, mothers all have to weigh things up. You too.

DO THIS

1. Think about all your options and actions carefully. Remember there's always a positive and a negative. Yin/Yang.
2. If one side isn't obvious, look more closely. It could be that NOT doing something might cost you in some way.
3. If you're confused or undecided on something, make lists on both sides.
4. You can also do the same for an alternative behaviour.
5. Be careful. And, even that has a cost/benefit too!

No. 32.

Yes, sleep is an ingredient of good mental and physical health. But stop thinking about how much you need or don't get. Relax. Get into a habit, breathe and let go. Sleep is a cruel paradox. The harder you try the worse it can get!

DO THIS

1. Firstly, please stop worrying about sleep. It will keep you awake. Ease the pressure.
2. Your body has a circadian rhythm – arise at the same time each day. Get some light into your eyes.
3. Not dropping off? Breathe in twice through your nose (once halfway then fully and deeply) and then sigh out. Repeat x 15.
4. Look into Tension Release Breathing – holding muscle groups whilst holding the breath and slowly releasing on the outbreath.

Stop
trying to sleep
And
Sleep

Living Wis

Chapter No. 4.

in
dom

Anger kills *you,* not *them*

No. 33.

'Holding onto anger is like drinking poison and expecting the other person to die' (Buddha). Work every day on recognising anger and allowing it to pass through you and you will become happier, healthier, calmer and a pleasure to hang out with.

DO THIS

1. Breathe in deeply, hold for 5.
2. Breathe out through your mouth slowly for 10.
3. Say quietly to yourself, 'Today I let go of regrets, grievances and resentments' ...
4. Breathe in 'love, forgiveness and acceptance'.
   Repeat 3 times. And be on alert throughout the day to anything arising! If it does, repeat the exercise.

No. 34.

Gratitude is one of the world's longest kept non-secrets. And it really works – because it refocuses you on what you have, not what you don't ... and puts things into perspective, whilst promoting good health and abundance.

DO THIS

1. Whatever you're going through, or have been through, keep a gratitude journal.
2. List what you're thankful for every night before bed and run them through your mind.
3. It could be the people who love you, who care about you, the job you have, the air you breathe. Anything. Think!
4. Look at the list when you wake for 5 minutes, breathe in each item and relax out.

The inestimable power of Gratitude

Change yourself first. Then the world

No. 35.

'Be the change you want to see in the world' (Gandhi). Most mystics and philosophers agree, change starts from within. As our views are often skewed by the lens of our own experience, we need to watch ourselves and what we think and do.

DO THIS

1. Get your own house in order. Keep working on yourself and your ego. Every day.

2. Every night, take a review of the day. Make notes: what could you have done better? How could you have responded better to a particular person?

3. Did you do any harm today or waste any time? Do better tomorrow and slowly carve a better you.

No. 36.

Letting go of things we cannot change is the key to peace and good mental health. The past, the news, other people and their behaviours or views. Learn to know what you really have the power to change. Starting perhaps with yourself.

DO THIS

1. Learn the Serenity prayer: 'God grant me the serenity to accept the things I cannot change; courage to change the things I can; and wisdom to know the difference'.

2. Stop and check in with yourself. Are you worrying about or annoyed by something you can't change?

3. Take a breath, let go and turn the thought around to see what you can actually do or say today that would make a positive difference to you or someone else.

Accept what you cannot Change

Practise Loving yourself and beyond

No. 37.

To love with freedom, without attachment, unconditionally, is real love. A love untainted by ego – unclutching, unceasing, unifying. Learning to love yourself is the first step towards loving authentically – not just for you, but for all.

DO THIS

1. Close your eyes and meditate on your kindness, moments of empathy, love and warmth.
2. Ponder times when you've been less than kind. Maybe selfish, critical and resentful.
3. Recognise that all the non-love in 2 above has been through fear, separation and our wrong-minded, ego-minded self.
4. Be kind and forgive yourself ... say, 'I love and fully accept myself for all my faults – knowing I am improving myself daily'. Expand beyond the ego.

No. 38.

Thomas Edison is credited with inventing the lightbulb. Famously, it took him 1000 attempts. But he said, 'I didn't fail 1000 times, the lightbulb was an invention with 1000 steps'. Take note and you can become amazing.

DO THIS

1. Never be frightened to make a mistake.
2. Whenever you say or hear the word, 'fail' or 'failure' instantly convert it to 'feedback'. It's how we move forward, invent things, create and inspire.
3. If you feel frozen before you attempt something (exams, in sport, a speech or creative endeavour), push on ... and 'fail' if you must. But remember that you had a go ... and you learned something: how NOT to do it that way.

Treat failure as feedback

FORGIVE
and *suffer*
no more

No. 39.

Forgiveness is the way out of emotional torture and separation. It dissolves differences and the past. It heralds a new start and promotes harmony. The highest spiritual act? Maybe. And maybe the toughest! But if we're to survive, we must try harder.

DO THIS

1. Has someone harmed, betrayed, rejected or insulted you? Sit with that for some minutes, quietly, with eyes closed. Feel the feeling, however strong.

2. Think back to things you might have done or said that have been hard for others to accept.

3. Breathe in, hold for 6 and allow ... then breathe out and through the emotion – and say to yourself, 'I forgive myself for this feeling, I forgive xxx for this and I will let go now'. Repeat until the feeling passes through you and releases. Keep practising this.

No. 40.

Sometimes we can be totally blinkered or over-focused – getting locked into one particular argument or idea at the expense of everything else. If we refuse to see another angle, expect untold mental anguish and discord.

DO THIS

1. If you're starting to be convinced of anything, of ANY kind, stop yourself right there.
2. Become AWARE and open yourself up to the opposite for a moment.
3. Ask yourself, 'What am I ignoring?' or 'What have I forgotten here?'
4. Think deeply. There's always another side to consider ... and it may have some value or merit.
5. You can do this in arguments. Over ANYTHING. It really helps the learning process.

What are you Ignoring?

Spread a *kindness* epidemic

No.41.

Sometimes we get lost in the competitiveness of life. The getting, earning, winning, forging ahead. And we forget that we're all in this together. So we can forget kindness too. How it works reciprocally – and is profoundly releasing.

DO THIS

1. Remember, you don't have to be Mother Teresa. Simple acts are always appreciated.
2. Smile at a stranger.
3. Have a conversation with someone lonely.
4. Giving is receiving, they say, so give something to someone daily and note what changes happen.
5. Do you have too much of everything? You might want to declutter – and find a more useful home for the excesses in your life.

No. 42.

'He's this'. 'She's that'. 'He's always shouting at her'. All the snap judgments and criticisms. Most of the time we know nothing about people's lives, what they're going through or even if we're seeing it clearly and objectively. Hold fire!

DO THIS

1. Bring some 360 degree understanding to the fore. It's that **Awareness** again.
2. Consider if you're projecting something that's actually in you onto them. After all, YOU were the one who re-cognised it (note that word!).
3. Stop before labelling someone, take that life-saving breath ... and think deeper.
4. Ask more questions, be inquisitive and keep an open mind.

STOP
the incessant
Judgment

Spirit
and **a littl**

Chapter No. 5.

uality
e magic

EGO
or *Infinite*
Consciousness?

No. 43.

It seems we can either be in the Ego mind or non-local, infinite consciousness (the part that never dies). The ego is the body and separation, where fear and insecurities arise. The other is oneness, love and unity. Where we act from is up to us.

DO THIS

1. Recognise feelings of fear, anger, resentment, anxiety or pride. You are in the ego mind.

2. Forgive yourself. You are among the 99.999%.

3. Accept and allow these feelings to move on. You may wish to meditate.

4. Expand towards Awareness, become the Observer and feel love, peace and (w)holiness. You'll help bring healing to yourself and the separation we most often experience.

No. 44.

The world is perfect. Yet you've always believed things need changing, people need changing, right? Wrong. Stop trying to change reality, demanding it be your way. Celebrate it all. Change yourself. Wake up ... and your world **will** change!

DO THIS

1. Identify the negative feelings in you. If you're not aware of them they will control you.

2. Check – are you wanting things your way? Realise that the feeling is likely in YOU, the fault is not outside. Remember to accept.

3. Never identify as that feeling. Never say, 'I AM depressed', 'I AM annoyed.' Rather say, 'IT is depressed' or, 'I am DOING annoyance'. Let it pass.

4. Know: when **you** change, everything changes.

How
to be constantly
happy

Becoming **Nature** again

No. 45.

Nature just does. Migration, hibernation, propagation. It all seems intimately synchronised, effortlessly flowing, with no interruptions. Joining in and letting go can be curiously soothing and wonderfully healing – like a homecoming.

DO THIS

1. Get out into a woodland area or somewhere in the country. Pick a suitable spot.
2. Stand still, close your eyes and silence your mind.
3. Listen for sounds – closely for a minute or so.
4. Pick up three objects nearby (e.g. a leaf, an acorn etc.) and really study them. Feel them on your skin.
5. If you want, sit down and draw the scene or objects quietly. Enjoy that you are part of infinite nature.

No. 46.

Synchronicity is super co-incidence – like when the person you're thinking of suddenly calls you. Gasp at these as signs of connection to a greater whole, know that you belong and that there's more between heaven and earth than you thought.

DO THIS

1. Pay close attention to the little things in your life as they emerge.
2. Zoom in on what people say, what you see revealing itself to you each day.
3. Notice little collisions, nudges and patterns.
4. Keep a journal of these and it'll happen more and more.
5. Know you're on a path, a journey, co-creating an expanded you.

Synchronicity
and the
OMG
factor

Your imagination is king.
Be careful!

No. 47.

Your imagination is the most powerful thing you have. It can get you into serious mental health trouble. Or it can unleash your genius. Harness this most unique of tools and you can create yourself a fabulously rich and joyful life.

DO THIS

1. Find a quiet place and close your eyes. Imagine an image of yourself in the near future as you would LIKE to be.
2. Think of the current difficulties you're facing and how you might solve them.
3. Describe your ideal future self in the present: 'I am ...' and add your words, in detail.
4. Take some breaths ... and picture yourself evolving from now into that person – with feeling. And repeat three times. Make this a daily habit.

No. 48.

Science has discovered we live in a quantum field, bathed in a sea of energy and light. It seems we may be able to co-create with the universe by meditating on our goals with clarity, assumption and feeling. Research more, with due diligence!

DO THIS

1. Practise being part of 'the light'. Close your eyes, breathe deeply and imagine a quiet lake of light in the centre of your mind ...
2. As you breathe in, it expands; breathe out and allow the light through your brain and body.
3. Be one with the light, then place an intention for your life. Imagine your goals really happening. Experience the 'interdependent co-arising'.

Co-create
USING THE
Quantum
Field

Mad, unwavering faith

No. 49.

Richard Branson, Winston Churchill, Elon Musk, Tom Cruise. Mad, crazy people, some ... but madly successful. It's about absolute certainty, motivation. A faith – in themselves or something higher. Get this spirit and anything is possible.

DO THIS

1. Read up on all the super successful people you admire; sports stars, pop stars, inventors, artists, business people. Especially the less privileged or less educated.

2. Research their books, posts or audios and investigate their methods and mental attitude.

3. Look at yourself in the mirror ... really look into your eyes and build that **belief.** Stick self-belief affirmations around on post-it-notes.

4. Make sure your belief is good, sound and ethical.

No. 50.

'I am ...' is the basis of our self-talk. It's our auto-suggestion or affirmation and, repeated, can become highly self-fulfilling. Be aware of what you unconsciously say. You don't want to manifest any negativity or block any abundance.

DO THIS

1. Make a recording of your own 'I am's ...'.
2. Make up some empowering suggestions like those opposite.
3. Before bed, before sleep, close your eyes, take some deep breaths and move your eyeballs upwards under the lids 30% ... and count down from 100 slowly.
4. Then listen to your recording as you drift downwards to sleep. Do this nightly as consistently as you can.

The power of I AM

- I am BEAUTIFUL
- I am EMPOWERED by POSITIVE INSPIRED thoughts
- I am LIGHT
- I am OPEN to ABUNDANCE
- I am THRIVING
- I am STABLE and CENTRED
- I am STRONG
- I am LOVE
- I am HEALTHY and WELL
- I am CAPABLE of ACHIEVING my dreams
- I am BOLD
- I am KIND and PATIENT
- I am untapped POTENTIAL
- I am CONNECTED to the earth beneath my FEET

'David is amazing ... he has changed my life ...'

— *Conor, UK (client)*

'... excellent in every aspect ... the sessions and exercises have improved my quality of life significantly ...'

— *TS, UK (client)*

'David has been fantastic with fixing my everyday anxieties – huge help with running a business ...'

— *BB, UK (client)*

'Excellent material ... the improvements in my career, relationships have been life-changing ...'

— *RH, UK (client)*

'... brilliant ... tailored solutions that you can take away ... big improvement in my anxiety and confidence levels ...'

— *Emma, London (client)*

David Osborn-Cook, author

BA, Dip CBH, Dip Clin.Hyp. NLP.Coach, GQHP, Reg GHR

David works as a Cognitive Behavioural Hypnotherapist and Life Coach with his own practice in Surrey, England. He specialises in helping clients with anxiety, stress and insomnia issues and runs workshops for companies and medical practices.

In a previous life he worked in the advertising and film industries as creative director, writer, executive producer and entrepreneur, and has founded and co-run his own marketing and video agencies.

He lives with his wife, Sarah and two cats, Cameron and Lola.

Contact him at **help@docwellness.co.uk**
visit **www.DOCwellness.co.uk**
or on instagram **@docwellnesshypno**

To explore more of the ideas in this book, look to the following, to whom I owe much thanks:

Eckhart Tolle, Aaron Beck, Albert Ellis, Carl Jung, Marcus Aurelius, Anthony De Mello, Byron Katie, Rupert Spira, Bruce Lipton, Rhonda Byrne, Joe Dispenza, Donald Hoffman, Bernardo Kastrup, Mooji, Deepak Chopra, Jean Houston, Neville Goddard, Jordan Peterson, Andrew Salter, Iain McGilchrist, Rupert Sheldrake, Wayne Dyer, Alan Watts, Alan H Cohen, Hal Elrod, Michael Singer, Ken Wapnick.

Thanks also to Phil Parker, Mark Davies, Bob Palmer, Paul Snoxell, Nick Rochford, Michelle Brackenborough and Robina Cowan.

Index

A
Abundance – 34, 50
Acceptance – 9, 12, 29, 33, 36, 37, 43
Adversity – 29
Affirmations – 30, 49, 50
Alert – 33
Anchoring – 5
Anger – 33, 43, 44
Anxiety –1, 2, 6, 9, 10, 11, 25, 43
Arguments – 40
Attachment – 37
Attention – 45, 46
Auto-pilot – 4
Auto-Suggestion – 50
Average – 26
Avoidance – 10
Awareness – 3, 9, 11, 15, 19, 23, 28, 40, 42, 43

B
Belief – 49
Benefit – 31
Betrayal – 39
Blinkered – 40
Bold – 19
Bored – 18
Branson (Richard) – 49
Breathe/breaths – 5, 10, 16, 32, 33, 34, 36, 39, 42, 47, 48, 50
Buddha – 33

C
Calmer – 2, 16
Career – 24
Catastrophising – 1
CBT – 7
Change – 35, 36, 44
Charisma – 20, 22
Churchill (Winston) – 49
Circadian Rhythm – 32
Co-creating – 46, 48
Co-incidence – 46
Commit – 26
Community – 24
Comparing – 14
Competitive/ness – 41
Confidence – 17, 19, 20, 21, 22
Conflict – 9
Connection – 46
Contented –30
Cost – 31
Courage – 36
Critical/Criticism – 20, 37, 42
Cruise (Tom) – 49

D
Decisions – 31
Declutter – 41
Defensive – 21
Depression – 1, 44
Desiderata – 19
Disappointment – 14
Disconnected – 27
Distortions – 1
Drudgery – 24

E
Economic uncertainty – 9
Edison – 38
Ego – 35, 37, 43
Ellis (Albert) – 7
Empathy – 37
Engage – 28
Environment – 9

Evolving – 47
Excesses – 41
Exercise – 30
Expectations – 7, 9, 12
Experience – 29
Expression – 17

F
Failure/failings – 23, 38
Faith – 49
Family – 24
Fear – 10, 12, 19, 37, 38, 43
Feedback – 38
Feel – 27
Flow/flowing – 16, 45
Forgiveness – 33, 37, 39, 43
4-3-2-1 – No.2
Friends – 24
Fun/Leisure – 24

G
Generalising – 1, 10
Genius – 47
Gandhi – 35
Giving and Receiving – 41
Goals – 23, 48
Gratitude – 25, 34
Gratitude Journal – 34
Gregorian Chant – 27
Grievances – 13, 33

H
Habits – 25, 30, 32, 47
Happy/Happiness – 44
Hardwired – 25
Healing – 27, 43, 45
Health/Well-being – 24
Hebb (Donald) – 25
Heroism – 29

Holiness – 43
Humility – 20
Hypnosis – 11

I
I am – 47, 49
Identity – 9
Ignoring – 40
Illusion – 13
Imagination – 10, 47, 48
Immunity – 12
Infinite Consciousness – 43
Infinite nature – 45
Information – 6
Inhibitions – 17
Inoculation – 12
Insecurity – 43
Intention – 48
Interdependent co-arising – 48
Interested – 28
Intrusive thoughts – 4
In vitro – 17
In vivo – 17

J
Journaling – 30, 34, 46
Judgment – 42

K
Kindness – 37, 41

L
Labelling – 42
Laughter – 20
Leaves on stream – 8
Light/The Light – 48
Love – 33, 34, 37, 43

M
Manifesting – 19, 50
Marriage – 24
Mastering – 18
Meaning – 13
Meditation – 8, 30, 37, 39, 48
Mindfulness – 7, 8, 13, 30
Mirroring – 28
Money – 24
Mother Theresa – 41
Motivation – 18, 49
Mozart – 27
Music – 27
Musk (Elon) – 49
Musturbation (must, need, should) – 7

N
Nature – 45
Negative Self Hypnosis – 11
Negative Thoughts –1, 4, 8, 9, 11
Neurons– 25
Neuroplasticity – 25
Neuroscience – 25
News – 6
The Now – 2, 23

O
Observer/Observing – 9, 19, 43

P
Paradox – 32
Parental pressure – 7
Patterns – 46
Peace – 36, 43
The Past – 2, 13, 23, 36
Peer pressure – 7
Personal Growth – 24
Perspective – 11

Pinching – 5
Positive thinking – 25
Powerful – 17
Pressures – 7, 12
Pride – 43
Projecting – 42
Public Speaking – 10, 17

Q
Q – Quantum Field – 48

R
Rap – 27
Rating thoughts – 1
Reading – 30
Reboot – 18
Re-centred – 2
Reframing – 15
Regrets – 13, 33
Rehearse – 17
Rejection – 39
Resentments – 33, 37, 43
Resilience – 12
Respect – 20
Rewiring – 25
Rumination – 13

S
School pressure – 7
Self-belief – 49
Self-conscious – 17, 19
Self-deprecating – 20
Self-esteem – 21
Selfish – 37
Self-fulfilling – 50
Self-Sabotaging – 4
Self-talk – 50
Self-worth – 20

Separation – 39, 43
Serenity Prayer – 36
Setbacks – 13
Shakespeare – 27
Shame – 20
Silence – 45
Sleep – 32
Slowing down – 22
Social Media pressure – 7
Speeches – 10, 17
Sub Conscious – 4, 7
Success/successful – 49
Suffering – 39
Social groups – 17
Story – 23
Successful – 30
Synchronicity – 46
Synchronised – 45

T
Tension Release Breathing – 32
Thankful – 34
Thoughts – 1, 2, 3, 4, 5, 8, 30
Thought Journal – 1, 30
Tracks of your Life – 27

U
Unenthusiastic – 18
Unfulfilled – 24
Unhappiness – 14
Universe – 48
Uplifts – 27

V
Values – 24
VIP – 28
Visualisation – 30

W
Wake up – 4
Watch yourself – 7, 35
What ifs – 2
Wheel of Life – 24
Whole-iness – 43, 46
Wisdom – 36
Woodland – 45
Worrying – 32
Worse (making things worse) – 3
Wrong-minded – 37

Y
Yin Yang – 31